GAYLORD F

Multiplying

Look out for these sections to help you learn more about each topic:

Remember...
This provides a summary of the key concept(s) on each two-page entry. Use it to revise what you have learned.

Word check
These are new and important words that help you understand the ideas presented on each two-page entry.

All of the word check entries in this book are shown in the glossary on page 45. The versions in the glossary are sometimes more extensive explanations.

Book link...
Although this book can be used on its own, other titles in the *Math Matters!* set may provide more information on certain topics. This section tells you which other titles to refer to.

Place value

To make it easy for you to see exactly what we are doing, you will find colored columns behind the numbers in all the examples on this and the following pages. This is what the colors mean:

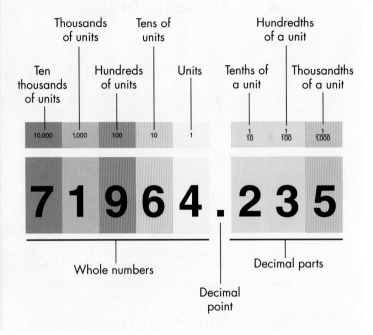

Thousands of units

Tens of units

Hundredths of a unit

Ten thousands of units

Hundreds of units

Units

Tenths of a unit

Thousandths of a unit

| 10,000 | 1,000 | 100 | 10 | 1 | $\frac{1}{10}$ | $\frac{1}{100}$ | $\frac{1}{1,000}$ |

7 1 9 6 4 . 2 3 5

Whole numbers

Decimal parts

Decimal point

Series concept by *Brian Knapp and Duncan McCrae*
Text contributed by *Brian Knapp and Colin Bass*
Design and production by *Duncan McCrae*
Illustrations of characters by *Nicolas Debon*
Digital illustrations by *David Woodroffe*
Other illustrations by *Peter Bull Art Studio*
Editing by *Lorna Gilbert and Barbara Carragher*
Layout by *Duncan McCrae and Mark Palmer*
Reprographics by *Global Colour*
Printed and bound by *LEGO SpA, Italy*

First Published in the United States in 1999 by Grolier Educational, Sherman Turnpike, Danbury, CT 06816

Copyright © 1999
Atlantic Europe Publishing Company Limited

Library of Congress Cataloging-in-Publication Data
Math Matters!
    p. cm.
    Includes indexes.
    Contents: v.1.Numbers — v.2.Adding — v.3.Subtracting — v.4.Multiplying — v.5.Dividing — v.6.Decimals — v.7.Fractions – v.8.Shape — v.9.Size — v.10.Tables and Charts — v.11.Grids and Graphs — v.12.Chance and Average — v.13.Mental Arithmetic
    ISBN 0–7172–9294–0 (set: alk. paper). — ISBN 0–7172–9295–9 (v.1: alk. paper). — ISBN 0–7172–9296–7 (v.2: alk. paper). — ISBN 0–7172–9297–5 (v.3: alk. paper). — ISBN 0–7172–9298–3 (v.4: alk. paper). — ISBN 0–7172–9299–1 (v.5: alk. paper). — ISBN 0–7172–9300–9 (v.6: alk. paper). — ISBN 0–7172–9301–7 (v.7: alk. paper). — ISBN 0–7172–9302–5 (v.8: alk. paper). — ISBN 0–7172–9303–3 (v.9: alk. paper). — ISBN 0–7172–9304–1 (v.10: alk. paper). — ISBN 0–7172–9305–X (v.11: alk. paper). — ISBN 0–7172–9306–8 (v.12: alk. paper). — ISBN 0–7172–9307–6 (v.13: alk. paper).

    1. Mathematics — Juvenile literature. [1. Mathematics.]
I. Grolier Educational Corporation.
QA40.5.M38   1998
510 — dc21   98–7404
                                                        CIP
                                                         AC

Contents

Introduction

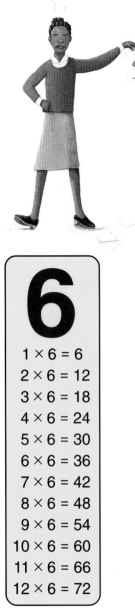

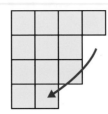

$$2 \times 2 = 4$$
$$3 \times 3 = 9$$
$$4 \times 4 = 16$$
$$5 \times 5 = 25$$

6

$1 \times 6 = 6$
$2 \times 6 = 12$
$3 \times 6 = 18$
$4 \times 6 = 24$
$5 \times 6 = 30$
$6 \times 6 = 36$
$7 \times 6 = 42$
$8 \times 6 = 48$
$9 \times 6 = 54$
$10 \times 6 = 60$
$11 \times 6 = 66$
$12 \times 6 = 72$

Multiplying is a fast way of adding. Multiplying saves time and effort adding many numbers of the same value (for example, **50** lots of **3**, or **28** lots of **4**).

Multiplication has a few basic rules, but it is also very flexible: you can multiply numbers in any order (multiplying **6** by **5** gives the same result as multiplying **5** by **6**, for example).

Once you have started to get comfortable with multiplication, you will find out about square numbers and square roots. Then you will see how to make a multiplication square. If you can learn the multiplication square, and the

$$(9 + 4) \times 8 = 13 \times 8$$

	10	4
8	80	32

×	1	2	3	4	5	6	7	8	9	10	11	12
1	1	2	3	4	5	6	7	8	9	10	11	12
2	2	4	6	8	10	12	14	16	18	20	22	24
3	3	6	9	12	15	18	21	24	27	30	33	36
4	4	8	12	16	20	24	28	32	36	40	44	48
5	5	10	15	20	25	30	35	40	45	50	55	60
6	6	12	18	24	30	36	42	48	54	60	66	72
7	7	14	21	28	35	42	49	56	63	70	77	84
8	8	16	24	32	40	48	56	64	72	80	88	96
9	9	18	27	36	45	54	63	72	81	90	99	108
10	10	20	30	40	50	60	70	80	90	100	110	120
11	11	22	33	44	55	66	77	88	99	110	121	132
12	12	24	36	48	60	72	84	96	108	120	132	144

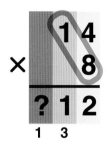

$$\begin{array}{r} 1\,4 \\ \times \quad 8 \\ \hline ?\,1\,2 \\ {\scriptstyle 1 \quad 3} \end{array}$$

1	2	3	4	5	6	7	8	9	10
11	12	13	14	15	16	17	18	19	20
21	22	23	24	25	26	27	28	29	30
31	32	33	34	35	36	37	38	39	40
41	42	43	44	45	46	47	48	49	50
51	52	53	54	55	56	57	58	59	60
61	62	63	64	65	66	67	68	69	70
71	72	73	74	75	76	77	78	79	80
81	82	83	84	85	86	87	88	89	90
91	92	93	94	95	96	97	98	99	100

$$4.70 \times 17 = ?$$

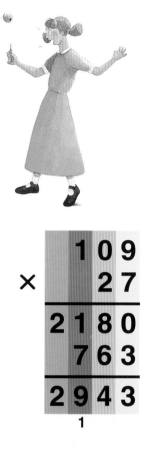

multiplication tables that follow, then you will find multiplication even faster.

You will find that by following the simple stages in this book, it will be easy to learn the ideas of multiplying. Each idea is set out on a separate page, so that you can quickly refer back to an idea if you have forgotten it.

Like all of the books in the *Math Matters!* set, there are many examples. They have been designed to be quite varied to show you that you can use mathematics at any time, any place, anywhere. Some of the examples are based on stories, so have fun reading them as you go.

$$\begin{array}{r} 1\,0\,9 \\ \times \quad 2\,7 \\ \hline 2\,1\,8\,0 \\ 7\,6\,3 \\ \hline 2\,9\,4\,3 \\ {\scriptstyle 1} \end{array}$$

×	1	2	3	4	5	6	7	8	9	10	11	12
1		2										
2	2	4	6	8	10	12	14	16	18	20	22	24
3		6					21					
4		8					28					
5		10										
6		12										
7		14	21	28								
8		16										
9		18										
10		20										
11		22										
12		24										

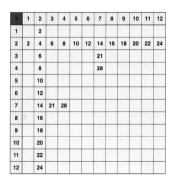

$$2 \times 8 = 16$$

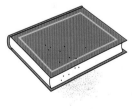

$$\begin{array}{r} 3\,8 \\ \times \quad 1\,4 \\ \hline 1\,5\,2 \\ 3\,8\,0 \\ \hline 5\,3\,2 \end{array}$$

Why multiply?

Multiplying is the same as adding the same numbers over and over again. You multiply to save time.

Adding many of the same thing is very common. For example, you may go into a shop and ask for six cartons of milk or eight snack bars. You could write out a list and start adding each item, but you don't have to. Instead, you multiply.

Here is an example of the kind of problem that multiplication makes easy, although you won't find out how easy until you turn to the next page...

Emily solves the problem

Emily's family were having three guests for the week: two aunts and an uncle. But the aunts and uncle had very fixed eating habits, and they each insisted on having a boiled egg for their breakfast. So they needed **3** eggs for each day.

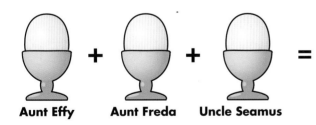 **= 3 eggs each day**

Aunt Effy   **Aunt Freda**   **Uncle Seamus**

Emily's mom knew that she didn't have enough eggs in the fridge for their needs for the whole week, so she suggested that Emily buy the eggs from the local farm shop. Now Emily had to work out how many eggs to buy.

Emily began by drawing out 3 eggs on a sheet of paper, grouping them in lines for each day of the week. Then she added the daily totals.

	Aunt Effy		Aunt Freda		Uncle Seamus		
Day 1	🥚	+	🥚	+	🥚	=	3
Day 2	🥚	+	🥚	+	🥚	=	3
Day 3	🥚	+	🥚	+	🥚	=	3
Day 4	🥚	+	🥚	+	🥚	=	3
Day 5	🥚	+	🥚	+	🥚	=	3
Day 6	🥚	+	🥚	+	🥚	=	3
Day 7	🥚	+	🥚	+	🥚	=	3
Total number of eggs required							**21**

By adding, Emily found that it took a long time to discover that she needed 21 eggs in the fridge before the visit.

But this is a very slow way of working things out. This is why we use multiplication. To find out how, turn the page.

Tip... It often helps to draw little pictures of what you are trying to do.

Remember... It is often possible to draw a picture when you don't know how to do a calculation. Once you can see the drawing, you can often see how to work it out.

Word check:
+ : The symbol for adding.
Adding: A quick way of counting.
Total: The answer to an adding problem.
Equals: The things on either side of an equals sign are the same.

How to multiply

Multiplying saves time by cutting down the numbers that we need to work with. The key to multiplying is to count rows and columns.

Here we use Emily's problem from page 6 and write it down a different way.

Counting rows and columns

Emily's drawing arranged the eggs into 7 rows each containing 3 eggs; that is, she had 7 rows and 3 columns. So Emily actually needed 7 lots of 3.

We already know that the total is 21 eggs. We can first write this down just as we might say it in conversation as:

7 lots of 3 makes 21

Now change the words <u>lots of</u> to <u>multiplied by</u> and <u>makes</u> to <u>equals</u>:

7 multiplied by 3 equals 21

Finally, we get the number equation:

$$7 \times 3 = 21$$

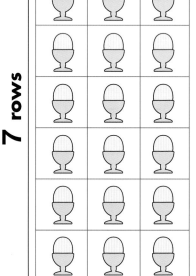

3 columns

7 rows

An extra visitor

Emily was just going out to buy the 21 eggs when the phone rang. It was another uncle saying he was coming to stay as well! So Emily was going to need more eggs.

But Emily was too smart to start counting from the beginning again because she already knew that $7 \times 3 = 21$

One extra person would need one egg for each day of the week, or 7 eggs, so the total was:

$21 + 7 = 28$

Which she could also write down as:

$7 + 7 + 7 + 7 = 28$

or:

$7 \times 4 = 28$

As you can see, the more adding there is to do, the more useful multiplication is!

Remember... Multiplication saves time. For example, $3 + 3 + 3 + 3$. There are 4 <u>of</u> <u>the</u> <u>same</u> numbers in this list, so we can write it as 4×3.

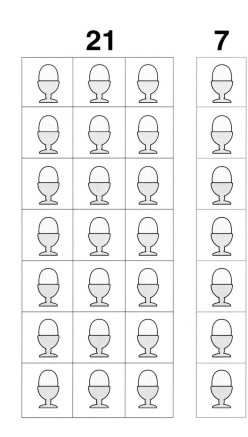

21   **7**

Word check

×: The symbol for multiplying. We say it "multiplied by" or "times."

= : The symbol for equals. We say it "equals" or "makes."

Column: Things placed one below the other.

Equation: A number sentence using the = symbol, telling us that two different ways of writing a number are the same. For example, $2 + 2 = 4$ and $9 - 5 = 4$.

Lots of: A common way of saying multiply.

Makes: A common word for equals.

Row: Things placed side by side.

You can multiply in any order

Many kinds of arithmetic need to be done in a strict order. This is not the case for multiplying: you can multiply numbers in any order. Let's see why multiplication works this way.

George's problem

George was curious to know if multiplying in any order really did give the same answer. So he put together a block of 12 squares.

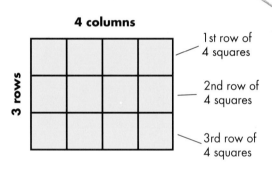

4 columns

3 rows

1st row of 4 squares

2nd row of 4 squares

3rd row of 4 squares

George knew that multiplication was done by multiplying rows and columns. In this case there were 3 rows and 4 columns.

3 rows of 4 columns makes 12

As on the previous page, the calculation could be written as:

$3 \times 4 = 12$

Rearranging and multiplying

Having done this, George decided to rearrange the squares as shown below:

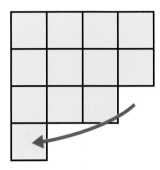 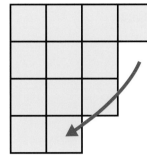 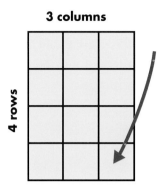

3 columns

4 rows

What he did was to move the blocks so that there were 4 rows and 3 columns. George then said to himself:

4 rows of 3 columns makes 12

Which he knew could be written as:

4 × 3 = 12

By doing this, George could see that whether you say four times three or three times four makes no difference. The answer is still twelve.

To check this, George then calculated 3 × 4 on his calculator, and finally 4 × 3. In both cases the answer he got was 12.

Remember… Like adding, you can multiply in any order without affecting the result.

And, by the way, George used a drawing to help him with the mathematics. The drawing made the mathematics easier to see.

Calculator check

You can do all of these calculations on a calculator as well.

All multiplication operations use the "×" symbol on the calculator. You enter one of the numbers, say 3, then press the multiplication sign (×), then enter the second number, say 4, and finally press the equals sign (=). The answer is then displayed. You can see this shown below.

Step 1: Enter 3
Step 2: Press multiplication sign (×)
Step 3: Enter 4
Step 4: Press equals sign (=)
(Answer 12)

Word check

Turn-Around Rule: When we add or multiply the same two numbers, the answer is the same no matter which of the numbers comes first (but it does not hold for subtracting or dividing).

Factors, multiples, and products

Every subject has its technical names, and mathematics is no exception. So here we have to think our way around three multiplication words… factor, multiple, and product.

Factor

This is the name for the numbers we multiply together. If we multiply 3 × 5, then both 3 and 5 are called factors.

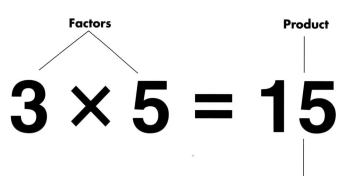

Factors

Product

$$3 \times 5 = 15$$

Multiple of 3 and 5

Multiple

All the numbers that can be obtained by multiplying by 3 are called multiples of 3. The first ones are 2 × 3 = 6; 3 × 3 = 9; 4 × 3 = 12; 5 × 3 = 15; and so on forever.

Describing a number like 117 as a multiple of 13 means that it comes from the list belonging to 13. To say that 13 is a factor of 117 is another way of saying the same thing.

Product

When we multiply two numbers (factors) together, we get an answer. When adding, we would use the word total. But when multiplying, the answer is called a product.

Here are some more examples:

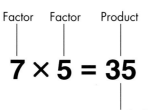

Factor   Factor   Product

$$7 \times 5 = 35$$

Multiple of 5 and 7

$$4 \times 8 = 32$$

Multiple of 4 and 8

$$2 \times 8 = 16$$

Multiple of 2 and 8

$$13 \times 9 = 117$$

Multiple of 13 and 9

Calculator check

You can do all of these calculations on a calculator as well. For example, 13×9, as shown below:

Step 1: Enter 13
Step 2: Press multiplication sign (×)
Step 3: Enter 9
Step 4: Press equals sign (=)
(Answer 117)

Remember... A product is made up of a pair of numbers multiplied together. A factor is the name for each of the numbers used in the multiplication.

Word check

Factor: A number used for multiplying.

Multiple: One of the numbers from the list of all products of the number.

Product: The answer when two or more numbers are multiplied together.

Prime numbers and prime factors

Some numbers are not multiples of smaller numbers. They are called prime numbers. When prime numbers are used as part of a multiplication, they are called prime factors. The prime numbers less than **20** are **2, 3, 5, 7, 11, 13, 17,** and **19**.

When multiplying, it is important to know that there are some special numbers called prime numbers. Prime numbers are the building numbers of multiplication. They cannot be split into combinations of two smaller numbers. For example, although the number 4 can be made by multiplying 2×2, the number 5 cannot be made by multiplying together any smaller whole numbers, and so it is a prime number. A prime factor is simply a prime number used in a multiplication.

Examples

Prime factors (a factor that cannot be made by multiplying together any smaller numbers).

Product (a number that is made by multiplying two smaller numbers).

$$3 \times 5 = 15$$

Both 3 and 5 are prime factors of 15 because both 3 and 5 are multiplied together to make 15, but neither 3 nor 5 can themselves be made from smaller whole numbers.

In a similar way the numbers 3 and 7 are prime factors of 21. Clearly, the product of a multiplication can never be a prime number because it is calculated from two factors.

Prime factor

$$3 \times 4 = 12$$

Multiple of 2, so not a prime factor.

Prime factors

$$3 \times 7 = 21$$

Finding prime numbers

You can find prime numbers up to any size simply by using a table made of all the numbers in order. This is called the Sieve of Eratosthenes, after its inventor. A table of numbers up to 100 is shown here with the prime numbers on the red squares.

1	2	3	4	5	6	7	8	9	10
11	12	13	14	15	16	17	18	19	20
21	22	23	24	25	26	27	28	29	30
31	32	33	34	35	36	37	38	39	40
41	42	43	44	45	46	47	48	49	50
51	52	53	54	55	56	57	58	59	60
61	62	63	64	65	66	67	68	69	70
71	72	73	74	75	76	77	78	79	80
81	82	83	84	85	86	87	88	89	90
91	92	93	94	95	96	97	98	99	100

Copy this table to see how it works. Start by circling 2, which is the smallest prime number (we don't use 1). Any multiple of 2 cannot be a prime number. So go on in jumps of 2, crossing out 4, 6, 8, 10, etc., to 100.

Now circle 3, the next smallest prime number. Any multiple of 3 cannot be a prime number. Move on in jumps of 3, crossing out 9, 15, 21, 27, etc.

And so we go on. Circle 5, then go in jumps of 5, crossing any uncrossed multiple (25, 35, etc.).

Circle 7, go in jumps of 7, crossing any uncrossed multiple (only 49 and 77 left).

And that completes the sieve. Every number left is a prime number.

Remember... Prime numbers are those that are not multiples of others (2, 3, 5, 7, etc.). Prime factors are the prime numbers used in multiplication (for example, 2 × 2 × 5 = 20; the prime factors are 2 and 5.

Word check

Prime factor: A prime number being used as a factor.

Prime number: A number that is not a multiple of anything.

Square numbers and square roots

When a whole number is multiplied by itself, for example, **4 × 4**, the result is called a square number.

There are some whole numbers that are special. These are called square numbers.

Every square number can be produced by multiplying a number by itself. For example, if we multiply 2 × 2, we get 4. In this example 4 is the square number.

The number used to make a square number in this way is called a square root. In the case of 2 × 2 = 4 the square root number of 4 is 2.

Similarly, multiplying 3 by itself makes 9. So 9 is the square number, and 3 is its square root.

Multiplying 4 by itself makes 16. So 16 is the square number, and 4 is its square root. Multiplying 5 by itself makes 25. So 25 is the square number, and 5 is its square root.

You can see these examples set out in shapes on the right.

Other factors in square numbers

Square numbers can often be obtained without using the square roots. For example, 6 × 6 = 36, but 36 is also 9 × 4. But each square number only has one square root, and it is always a whole number.

▼ **Examples of square numbers and their square roots.**

Square roots

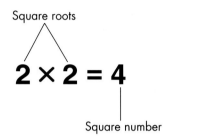

$$2 \times 2 = 4$$

Square number

$$3 \times 3 = 9$$

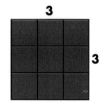

$$4 \times 4 = 16$$

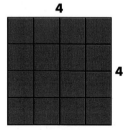

$$5 \times 5 = 25$$

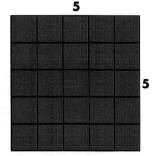

Square roots of other numbers

Every number has a square root, although only square numbers have square roots that are whole numbers. For example, 15 is a whole number, but it is not a square number because it is not the product of a number multiplied by itself.

The square root of 15 is therefore not a whole number. Using a calculator, you would find that the square root of 15 is:

$$3.8729833$$

Factors but not a square root

A product but not a square number

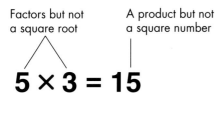

$$5 \times 3 = 15$$

Remember… The square root of a square number is always a whole number.

Word check

Square number: The number of a collection of objects that can be arranged in a square. It is the product of two equal numbers (for example, 16 is the square number produced from 4×4).

Square root: The number that, multiplied by itself, produces a square number.

Finding a square root using a calculator

Many calculators have buttons that will calculate square roots automatically. Every positive number has a square root, but only some have square roots that are whole numbers.

You can use your calculator to experiment to find out which numbers have exact square roots. For example, if you enter the number 36 and press the square root sign, the answer is 6 exactly. So 6 is an exact square root of 36, and 36 is a square number.

However, if the number 15 had been entered, the answer would have been 3.8729… This is clearly not a whole number, so 15 does not have an exact square root number. 15 is therefore not a square number either.

Step 1. Enter 36
Step 2. Press square root sign ($\sqrt{\ }$)
(Answer reads 6)

Starting a multiplication square

There is no quick way to work out the results of multiplication, and for most of us the most efficient thing we can do is learn some <u>multiplication facts</u> by heart.

Why a number square is useful

Multiplication facts are usually set out in the form of a square or as columns of numbers called <u>multiplication tables</u>, as shown on page 22.

We are going to start to build a multiplication square using some of the numbers we obtained on the previous pages.

For example, on pages 8 and 9 we learned:

$7 \times 3 = 21$ and $7 \times 4 = 28$

On page 10 we also learned the Turn-Around Rule, so that

$7 \times 3 = 3 \times 7 = 21$

and

$7 \times 4 = 4 \times 7 = 28$

These four facts have been placed into a diagram that will build into a square-shaped table.

This table is made by writing the numbers 1 to 12 down the page and then across the page, as you can see above.

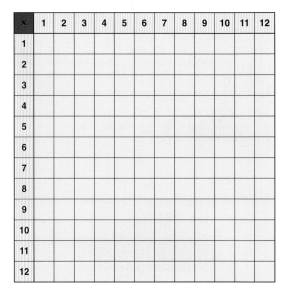

×	1	2	3	4	5	6	7	8	9	10	11	12
1												
2												
3												
4												
5												
6												
7												
8												
9												
10												
11												
12												

Finding your way around in the multiplication square

Step 1: Choose the first number from the left column, and put your finger on it. In this case we have selected 7, and it has been marked with a green circle.

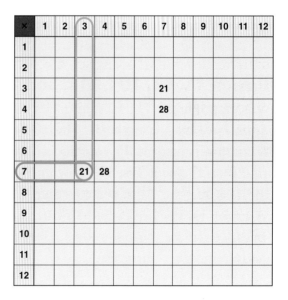

×	1	2	3	4	5	6	7	8	9	10	11	12
1												
2												
3							21					
4							28					
5												
6												
7			21	28								
8												
9												
10												
11												
12												

Step 2: Choose the second number from the top row and put another finger on it. In this case we have selected 3, and it has been marked with a blue circle.

Step 3: Run one finger down from the number top row and the other across from the number in the left column until they meet. This is where we find the answer, 21.

×	1	2	3	4	5	6	7	8	9	10	11	12
1												
2												
3							21					
4							28					
5												
6												
7			21	28								
8												
9												
10												
11												
12												

Remember... Knowing the Turn-Around Rule has already cut your learning almost in half. This is how we have been able to put four numbers on the square on this page when we have only worked out two results! The same is true for all other pairs of numbers.

Word check

Multiplication facts: The numbers produced by multiplying together numbers we use a lot, such as $3 \times 4 = 12$. They are facts we remember rather than work out each time. Some people also refer to these multiplication facts as multiplication tables.

Multiplication square: The multiplication tables arranged into a square shape.

Multiplication tables: Multiplication facts set out in columns.

Completing the multiplication square

Much of the multiplication square can be completed by filling in more easy facts. Some examples of these are shown here. Filling in the square like this is useful because it shows you which numbers do not form parts of easy-to-learn patterns. These awkward numbers are shown in red on the page opposite.

Filling in 2's

The 2's row and column was done by simply adding a number to itself. For example, 2×7 is the same as $7 + 7$. The answer is 14

Filling in 1's, 6's, 10's, 11's, and 12's

In this example the 1's, 10's, and 11's row and column have been completed. The 10's row and column is just the 1's row and column with a 0 on the end. The 11's row and column is the 10's and the 1's added together.

   A dozen means 12, and a half-dozen means 6. Because we use these numbers a lot, we quickly remember answers.

Filling in 5's and square numbers

Multiples of 5 all end in 5 or 0. We have done the square numbers already on page 16.

Filling in results from page 10

$4 \times 3 = 12$
$3 \times 4 = 12$

▼ The multiplication square with 2's inserted.

×	1	2	3	4	5	6	7	8	9	10	11	12
1		2										
2	2	4	6	8	10	12	14	16	18	20	22	24
3		6					21					
4		8					28					
5		10										
6		12										
7		14	21	28								
8		16										
9		18										
10		20										
11		22										
12		24										

▼ The multiplication square with 1's, 6's, 10's, 11's, and 12's inserted.

×	1	2	3	4	5	6	7	8	9	10	11	12
1	1	2	3	4	5	6	7	8	9	10	11	12
2	2	4	6	8	10	12	14	16	18	20	22	24
3	3	6				18	21			30	33	36
4	4	8				24	28			40	44	48
5	5	10				30				50	55	60
6	6	12	18	24	30	36	42	48	54	60	66	72
7	7	14	21	28		42				70	77	84
8	8	16				48				80	88	96
9	9	18				54				90	99	108
10	10	20	30	40	50	60	70	80	90	100	110	120
11	11	22	33	44	55	66	77	88	99	110	121	132
12	12	24	36	48	60	72	84	96	108	120	132	144

▼ The multiplication square with 5's, squared numbers, and numbers from page 10.

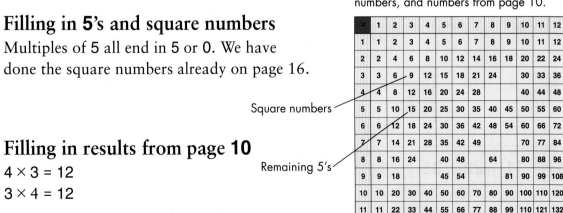

×	1	2	3	4	5	6	7	8	9	10	11	12
1	1	2	3	4	5	6	7	8	9	10	11	12
2	2	4	6	8	10	12	14	16	18	20	22	24
3	3	6	9	12	15	18	21	24		30	33	36
4	4	8	12	16	20	24	28			40	44	48
5	5	10	15	20	25	30	35	40	45	50	55	60
6	6	12	18	24	30	36	42	48	54	60	66	72
7	7	14	21	28	35	42	49			70	77	84
8	8	16	24		40	48		64		80	88	96
9	9	18			45	54			81	90	99	108
10	10	20	30	40	50	60	70	80	90	100	110	120
11	11	22	33	44	55	66	77	88	99	110	121	132
12	12	24	36	48	60	72	84	96	108	120	132	144

Square numbers

Remaining 5's

The finished square

Many people find these numbers difficult to learn, so be sure to concentrate on remembering them!

Remember... The multiplication square is made up of simple multiplication facts, as you can see.

▼ The multiplication square showing the numbers that people find difficult to learn.

×	1	2	3	4	5	6	7	8	9	10	11	12
1	1	2	3	4	5	6	7	8	9	10	11	12
2	2	4	6	8	10	12	14	16	18	20	22	24
3	3	6	9	12	15	18	21	24	27	30	33	36
4	4	8	12	16	20	24	28	32	36	40	44	48
5	5	10	15	20	25	30	35	40	45	50	55	60
6	6	12	18	24	30	36	42	48	54	60	66	72
7	7	14	21	28	35	42	49	56	63	70	77	84
8	8	16	24	32	40	48	56	64	72	80	88	96
9	9	18	27	36	45	54	63	72	81	90	99	108
10	10	20	30	40	50	60	70	80	90	100	110	120
11	11	22	33	44	55	66	77	88	99	110	121	132
12	12	24	36	48	60	72	84	96	108	120	132	144

▼ The complete multiplication square.

×	1	2	3	4	5	6	7	8	9	10	11	12
1	1	2	3	4	5	6	7	8	9	10	11	12
2	2	4	6	8	10	12	14	16	18	20	22	24
3	3	6	9	12	15	18	21	24	27	30	33	36
4	4	8	12	16	20	24	28	32	36	40	44	48
5	5	10	15	20	25	30	35	40	45	50	55	60
6	6	12	18	24	30	36	42	48	54	60	66	72
7	7	14	21	28	35	42	49	56	63	70	77	84
8	8	16	24	32	40	48	56	64	72	80	88	96
9	9	18	27	36	45	54	63	72	81	90	99	108
10	10	20	30	40	50	60	70	80	90	100	110	120
11	11	22	33	44	55	66	77	88	99	110	121	132
12	12	24	36	48	60	72	84	96	108	120	132	144

Multiplication tables

Multiplication facts can be set out as a square and also in the form of a columns of numbers called multiplication tables. It is easier to see patterns in multiplication squares. But multiplication tables are easier to learn by heart. Your aim should be to give the correct answer to any multiplication fact up to 12 × 12 without having to think.

▼ 12 × 12 square

×	1	2	3	4	5	6	7	8	9	10	11	12
1	1	2	3	4	5	6	7	8	9	10	11	12
2	2	4	6	8	10	12	14	16	18	20	22	24
3	3	6	9	12	15	18	21	24	27	30	33	36
4	4	8	12	16	20	24	28	32	36	40	44	48
5	5	10	15	20	25	30	35	40	45	50	55	60
6	6	12	18	24	30	36	42	48	54	60	66	72
7	7	14	21	28	35	42	49	56	63	70	77	84
8	8	16	24	32	40	48	56	64	72	80	88	96
9	9	18	27	36	45	54	63	72	81	90	99	108
10	10	20	30	40	50	60	70	80	90	100	110	120
11	11	22	33	44	55	66	77	88	99	110	121	132
12	12	24	36	48	60	72	84	96	108	120	132	144

You can see that the multiplication tables are simply parts of the multiplication square by looking at the 7 times table:

▶ This shows you how the 7 times table is related to a multiplication square.

This is the column used to make the 7 times table.

$$1 \times 7 = 7$$
$$2 \times 7 = 14$$
$$3 \times 7 = 21$$
$$4 \times 7 = 28$$
$$5 \times 7 = 35$$
$$6 \times 7 = 42$$
$$7 \times 7 = 49$$
$$8 \times 7 = 56$$
$$9 \times 7 = 63$$
$$10 \times 7 = 70$$
$$11 \times 7 = 77$$
$$12 \times 7 = 84$$

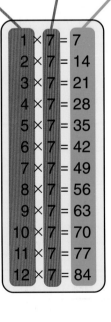

Remember… Multiplication tables are a separated-out form of a multiplication square. A multiplication square and the Turn-Around Rule help you understand that you only have to learn about half as many numbers as are in multiplication tables.

Here, for reference, are the multiplication tables for numbers from 2 to 12.

2
1 × 2 = 2
2 × 2 = 4
3 × 2 = 6
4 × 2 = 8
5 × 2 = 10
6 × 2 = 12
7 × 2 = 14
8 × 2 = 16
9 × 2 = 18
10 × 2 = 20
11 × 2 = 22
12 × 2 = 24

3
1 × 3 = 3
2 × 3 = 6
3 × 3 = 9
4 × 3 = 12
5 × 3 = 15
6 × 3 = 18
7 × 3 = 21
8 × 3 = 24
9 × 3 = 27
10 × 3 = 30
11 × 3 = 33
12 × 3 = 36

4
1 × 4 = 4
2 × 4 = 8
3 × 4 = 12
4 × 4 = 16
5 × 4 = 20
6 × 4 = 24
7 × 4 = 28
8 × 4 = 32
9 × 4 = 36
10 × 4 = 40
11 × 4 = 44
12 × 4 = 48

5
1 × 5 = 5
2 × 5 = 10
3 × 5 = 15
4 × 5 = 20
5 × 5 = 25
6 × 5 = 30
7 × 5 = 35
8 × 5 = 40
9 × 5 = 45
10 × 5 = 50
11 × 5 = 55
12 × 5 = 60

6
1 × 6 = 6
2 × 6 = 12
3 × 6 = 18
4 × 6 = 24
5 × 6 = 30
6 × 6 = 36
7 × 6 = 42
8 × 6 = 48
9 × 6 = 54
10 × 6 = 60
11 × 6 = 66
12 × 6 = 72

7
1 × 7 = 7
2 × 7 = 14
3 × 7 = 21
4 × 7 = 28
5 × 7 = 35
6 × 7 = 42
7 × 7 = 49
8 × 7 = 56
9 × 7 = 63
10 × 7 = 70
11 × 7 = 77
12 × 7 = 84

8
1 × 8 = 8
2 × 8 = 16
3 × 8 = 24
4 × 8 = 32
5 × 8 = 40
6 × 8 = 48
7 × 8 = 56
8 × 8 = 64
9 × 8 = 72
10 × 8 = 80
11 × 8 = 88
12 × 8 = 96

9
1 × 9 = 9
2 × 9 = 18
3 × 9 = 27
4 × 9 = 36
5 × 9 = 45
6 × 9 = 54
7 × 9 = 63
8 × 9 = 72
9 × 9 = 81
10 × 9 = 90
11 × 9 = 99
12 × 9 = 108

10
1 × 10 = 10
2 × 10 = 20
3 × 10 = 30
4 × 10 = 40
5 × 10 = 50
6 × 10 = 60
7 × 10 = 70
8 × 10 = 80
9 × 10 = 90
10 × 10 = 100
11 × 10 = 110
12 × 10 = 120

11
1 × 11 = 11
2 × 11 = 22
3 × 11 = 33
4 × 11 = 44
5 × 11 = 55
6 × 11 = 66
7 × 11 = 77
8 × 11 = 88
9 × 11 = 99
10 × 11 = 110
11 × 11 = 121
12 × 11 = 132

12
1 × 12 = 12
2 × 12 = 24
3 × 12 = 36
4 × 12 = 48
5 × 12 = 60
6 × 12 = 72
7 × 12 = 84
8 × 12 = 96
9 × 12 = 108
10 × 12 = 120
11 × 12 = 132
12 × 12 = 144

Short multiplication

This is a method of multiplying two numbers when one of them is **9** or less. It is called short multiplication.

The multiplication problem is normally set out in a row. But it is not easy to do a multiplication with the numbers arranged this way. It is much easier if we first organize the numbers into columns. To help you keep track of the values of each column, they have been given colors. For more information on the colored columns, see page 2.

The village party

Sarah was going to give out invitations for a party to be held in the village hall. The hall had **14** tables that would each seat **8** guests. So Sarah had to find out the number of guests she could invite. For this she used short multiplication.

Step 1: Write one number above the other, and line them both up on the right in columns.

Draw a line below them. The product, or answer, of the multiplication is then written below the line.

In this example we are multiplying 14 × 8, and so we write 8 below the 4 in 14. This is because both the 4 and the 8 are units (remember that 14 is actually 1 ten and 4 units).

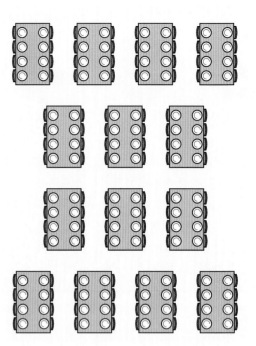

▼ **The problem written as a row**

$$14 \times 8 = ?$$

▼ **The same problem rearranged and placed onto colored columns.**

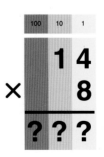

100	10	1
	1	4
×		8
?	?	?

Step 2: Start on the right, in the units column.

4 multiplied by 8 makes 32 (remember your multiplication tables!).

Since 32 is 3 tens and 2 units, write down 2 in the units column as part of the answer, and carry 3 below the tens column.

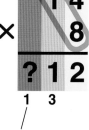

This is the 3 tens being carried.

Step 3: Now multiply the tens column. In this case multiply 1 by 8, giving the answer 8.

However, we must add the 3 that was carried from step 1. 8 + 3 = 11.

Write down 1 in the tens column, and carry 1 into the hundreds column.

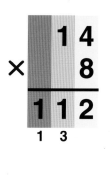

This is the 1 hundred being carried.

Step 4: Since there are no hundreds to multiply by 8, the carried 1 can be written in the hundreds column to complete the answer.

Sarah can invite 112 people to the party.

Remember... Follow the rules. Put one number above the other, lining them up on the right using columns. In short multiplication, multiply the larger number by the number with a single digit.

Word check

Carrying: In adding or multiplying, when the working column total is bigger than 10, this is the method of adding the left digit at the bottom of the column on the left.

Digit: The numerals 1, 2, 3, 4, 5, 6, 7, 8, 9, or 0. Several may be used to stand for a larger number. They are called digits to make it clear that they are only part of a complete number.

Other kinds of short multiplication

As in most mathematics, there are usually a variety of ways to solve a problem. This is what Narindar and Sargeet discovered when they wanted to find out the number of guests they could fit into a friend's restaurant. The problem is the same one that Sarah had on the previous page, but the answer is laid out in two different patterns.

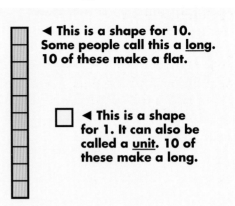

◄ This is a shape for 10. Some people call this a **long**. 10 of these make a flat.

◄ This is a shape for 1. It can also be called a **unit**. 10 of these make a long.

Example 1: Split up the problem

Multiplying 14 × 8 seemed hard to Narindar, so he solved the problem in a different way, using shapes.

He could see that 14 is made up of one 10 and 4 units, as shown on the right.

And Narindar knew that it was easy to multiply 10 × 8 and 4 × 8:

10 × 8 = 80
4 × 8 = 32

All he now needed to do was add these numbers:

14 × 8 = 112

What Narindar did was split up the problem into manageable parts. The shapes on this page show you how to think about the problem this way.

14 is made up of		
1 ten = 10	and	4 units = 4

Example 2: Using grids

Sargeet, a friend of Narindar, knew yet another way.

14

14 set out as a 10 and 4

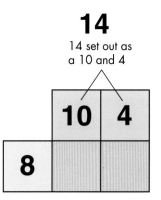

Step 1: By setting out the 14 as 10 + 4 in columns and the 8 as a row, he could make the multiplying easier.

Step 2: Next he multiplied the 10 by the 8 and wrote 80 below the ten. Then he multiplied 8 by the 4 and wrote 32 below the 4.

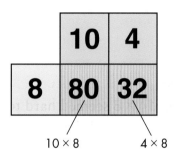

10×8 4×8

Step 3: Finally, he simply added 80 and 32 to get 112.

80 + 32 = 112

Remember... There are many ways of doing multiplication. You can separate a multiplication into easy parts and then add the answers, or you can set out your numbers in grids and multiply each pair of numbers to complete the grid. Then add these answers.

By the way... Now you have seen three ways of working out a simple multiplication (including the method on page 24). You can choose which one suits you best.

Book link... Find out more about ideas like this in the book *Mental Arithmetic* in the *Math Matters!* set.

Multiplying and adding

Sometimes problems involve both multiplying and adding. In this case we <u>do</u> have to do them in the right order. Here you see how Ziggie was clever in tackling this kind of problem.

Also... When people are tourists, they often have difficulty figuring out money in a foreign currency. Ziggie had to get used to £ sterling as well as multiplying and adding!

Ziggie and the crown jewels

Ziggie, her mother and father, and her five brothers and sisters went to visit the Tower of London. They arrived at the gate and found that the cost of entry was £9. But they also wanted to see the crown jewels, which were in the Bloody Tower, where many years ago lots of famous people were locked up before being executed. For this they had to pay an extra £4. While they waited in the line, Ziggie tried to help her father work out what he would have to pay when he got to the cashier.

Setting out the problem

Ziggie's father had to pay £9 and £4 for each of the eight people in his family. How much did he have to pay altogether? To find the answer, he had to add two separate multiplications:

Note: The £ sign before a number means pounds in the UK.

Cost of entry to the Tower of London

$$8 \times 9 = ?$$

The number of people in the group

The total needed for the cashier

$$8 \times 4 = ?$$

Cost of entry to the crown jewels

Multiplying then adding

Using her multiplication tables (which Ziggie had learned by heart at school, but which are also on page 23):

$$8 \times 9 = 72$$

and

$$8 \times 4 = 32$$

so

$$72 + 32 = 104$$

Adding then multiplying

Ziggie thought it would be easier to work it out like this:

Each person had to pay £9 and £4, so:

$$9 + 4 = 13$$

and

$$8 \times 13 = 104$$

Calculating in her head

Since Ziggie was standing in a line, she wanted to be able to work out the answer in her head. Since 9 + 4 is the same as 10 + 3, she could split her problem into:

$$8 \times 10 = 80$$

and

$$8 \times 3 = 24$$

so

$$80 + 24 = 104$$

Ziggie's father had to pay £104.

Book link... Find out more about calculating in your head in the book *Mental Arithmetic* in the *Math Matters!* set.

Using parentheses in multiplying

Parentheses are an important mathematical tool. They are used when we want to do things in an unusual order. Whatever is inside the parentheses <u>must</u> be done first.

Why parentheses are used

Ziggie's problem from page 28 involves multiplication and addition.

Normally, you <u>must</u> do the multiplication before the addition. Since Ziggie wanted to do the addition first, she needed to use parentheses. Instead of working out:

$$8 \times 9 + 8 \times 4 = 72 + 32 = 104$$

Ziggie saw that **8** was used in both multiplications, and so she wanted to add **9 + 4** first, then multiply the total by **8**.

Written out using parentheses, this is what Ziggie did:

$$(9 + 4) \times 8$$

Notice here that we are using the parentheses to tell us to do the addition first.

Because **8** is used in both multiplications, Ziggie was able to take it outside the parentheses.

Following the rule of doing whatever is inside the parentheses first, the calculation is:

$$(9 + 4) = 13$$
$$13 \times 8 = 104$$

The method Ziggie used on page 29 is called the <u>Splitting-Up Rule</u>.

Using brackets again

Let's have another look at what Ziggie did in her head (page 29).

$$(9 + 4) \times 8 = 13 \times 8$$

But Ziggie did not know her multiplication facts as far as 13 (not many people do). So this is what she did next.

She thought:

$$13 = 10 + 3$$

so she needed to work out:

$$(10 + 3) \times 8 = 10 \times 8 + 3 \times 8$$

This is easier to do because they are both easy multiplication facts.

Notice that this is another use of the Splitting-up Rule.

$$(10 \times 8) + (3 \times 8)$$
$$= 80 + 24$$
$$= 104$$

Remember... Parentheses are used when we want to make the order in which we do our arithmetic very clear. The problem inside the parentheses is done first.

Word check

Splitting-Up Rule: When two numbers are being multiplied, one of them can be split up into parts that are easier to multiply separately. The separate answers are then added together.

Long multiplication using grids

When numbers above **9** are multiplied together, you need to use a method called long multiplication. Here is one method that uses a grid. Other methods are shown on the following pages.

Problem

Wendy had been stacking cans of soup on a high supermarket display shelf. The stack looked very impressive, but then the manager asked her how many she had used so that he could keep a proper record of stock in the supermarket.

Wendy could have counted the cans, but that would have been very tedious. Since the cans were stacked up in rows, she knew that it would be much faster to count the rows and columns of the display and then multiply these two numbers together.

She quickly counted up the number of rows as **14** and the number of columns as **38**. But then she had to multiply them together:

$$14 \times 38 = ?$$

Step 1: Separate the numbers so they are easier to work with.

14 is 10 + 4

38 is 30 + 8

Step 2: Place the separated numbers in a grid as we did for short multiplication on page 27. Notice that in this case there are 2 rows because the number we are multiplying with has 2 digits.

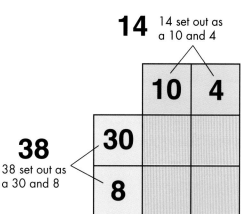

14 set out as a 10 and 4

38 set out as a 30 and 8

Step 3: Multiply the numbers together to fill in the squares. In this example we have multiplied 10 × 30, and the answer is 300.

Here you can see all of the squares filled in (8 × 10 = 80; 30 × 4 = 120; 8 × 4 = 32).

Step 4: Last of all, add all the numbers in the dark-shaded squares:

300 + 120 + 80 + 32 = 532

So Wendy had stacked 532 cans in the display.

Remember... You can use grids to multiply big numbers together, but first separate the numbers into tens, units, etc. When the grid is filled in, just add the numbers in the dark-shaded squares of the grid to find the total.

Long multiplication by columns

One way of doing long multiplication was shown on the previous page. Here is another method that uses columns to help guide you through the problem, as we did on page 24.

$$14 \times 38 = ?$$

Step 1: For long multiplication using columns place one number above the other, lining up the numbers on the right so that units line up with units, tens line up with tens, and so on. Draw a line below the numbers. The answer will go below this line.

100	10	1
	3	8
×	1	4
?	?	?

Step 2: We will multiply each part of the top number by each of the digits of the lower number in turn.

    If we start with the units from the bottom number, we say that $4 \times 8 = 32$, so we write **2** in the units column and carry a small **3** below the tens column, to add to the tens when we have worked them out.

This is the 3 tens carried over.

Step 3: Now we multiply the 3 by the 4 (3 × 4 = 12). Adding the carried over 3 makes a total of 15. Write 5 in the tens column and carry forward a small 1 into the hundreds column.

In fact, there are no other hundreds, so this 1 can be written next to the 5, making 152.

This is the 1 hundred carried over.

Step 4: Repeat the multiplication, this time with the 1 from the bottom row. This 1 is a ten, so we start by putting a 0 in the units column because there cannot be any units when we multiply by a ten.

Step 5: Working from the right, 1 × 8 = 8. Write this in the tens column. Moving left again, 1 × 3 = 3. Put this in the hundreds column, making 380.

We have now finished the multiplying, and we simply have two rows of the answer to add, giving the answer 532.

Remember... Line up the numbers on the right, one below the other. Start with the units, and do a short multiplication. Move on to the tens, put a zero on the right of the line below, and do another short multiplication. Then add the results.

Tip... It doesn't matter which number goes on top because of the Turn-Around Rule. But the number 1 is an easy number to multiply with, so in this case it helps to have it on the bottom line.

Multiplying large numbers using grids

Three-digit numbers can be multiplied using hidden columns or a grid. Here is how to do it with a grid.

Scare at Woodworm's bookshop

Woodworm's bookshop had some books in their stock that had not sold for years. One day the assistant was looking through one of these books, and she discovered that they really had woodworm eating the books.

Clearly they had to find out how many books had been lost. The old books were neatly packed against a wall. The assistant began counting, but then the manager came along and suggested a faster way using multiplication.

There were **468** columns of books, each stacked **79** books high.

The manager explained that it would be easiest first to separate the difficult numbers into something easier, like this:

468 = 400 + 60 + 8

and

79 = 70 + 9

After this a grid could be made up. He showed the assistant how to do it, like this:

468
This is 468 set out as 400, 60, and 8.

	400	60	8
70			
9			

79 This is 70 set out as a 70 and 9.

He then filled in one of the squares for her, using the multiplication tables he had memorized (if you haven't memorized yours, then remember they are on page 23). In this case he used the fact that 8 × 7 = 56, then remembered the number was 70, not 7, and so added a 0 to his answer.

	400	60	8
70			560
9			

8 × 70

Here you can see all of the squares filled in. Check they are correct by using the multiplication square on page 21 or the tables on page 23.

	400	60	8
70	28,000	4,200	560
9	3,600	540	72

All the assistant had to do now was add all the numbers in the squares. The addition is shown on the right. The answer was 36,972.

Remember... How to multiply large numbers by using grids. Break the large numbers into simpler numbers, then complete the grid as shown here.

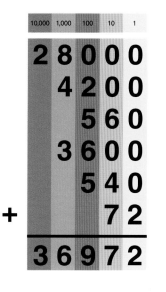

10,000	1,000	100	10	1
2	8	0	0	0
	4	2	0	0
		5	6	0
	3	6	0	0
		5	4	0
			7	2
3	6	9	7	2

+

Tip... If you have to multiply big numbers such as 70, try to find an easy way. In this case multiply by 7, and then add 0 to the answer.

Multiplying large numbers using columns

Long multiplication is simply many short multiplications added together. You can use as many hidden columns as you need to multiply really big numbers.

More than he expected!

Gavin had a wall along one side of his garden, and he wanted to build another one to match it. But to do so, he had to order the bricks first. Gavin needed to know how many bricks to order.

To find out, Gavin first dug down beside the existing wall to find out how many levels of bricks were below the surface. He discovered that there were seven levels. Then he counted up the levels above the ground and found there were **20** more levels (builders call these levels "courses").

Next, he walked along the wall counting the numbers of bricks in the top course. He could have chosen any other course, since they all contain the same number of bricks, but the top one was easiest. He found that there were **109** bricks in the top course.

Gavin could now work out how many bricks to order by multiplying the number of bricks in the length (109) by the number in the height (27).

Here is the problem written out as a long multiplication using the method on page 34. However, in this case we will multiply by the tens first and the units last.

109 × 27 = ?

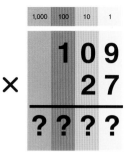

Step 1: Multiply by 20.

Put a 0 in the right-hand column and multiply the top row by 2.

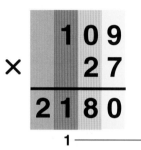

1 —— This is the 1 hundred carried over.

Tip... When doing long multiplication, always put the right-hand digit of each answer directly below the digit you are multiplying by.

Step 2: Multiply by 7.

Start a new row for the answer. Multiply the top row by 7.

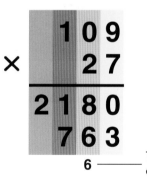

6 —— This is the 6 tens carried over.

Step 3: Add the results.

Answer: Gavin needs to order 2,943 bricks.

Remember... To choose a method that suits you. Here you can see that you can multiply long numbers directly, line by line, or you can split the numbers up and make them easier to multiply. Choose whichever method suits you – they all give the same answer, of course!

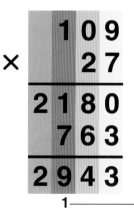

1 —— This is the 1 hundred carried over.

Multiplying decimal numbers

Decimals show whole numbers and parts of numbers. A period is placed after the units so that we will know which one it is. The period is called a decimal point.

Just as with whole numbers, which have the smallest on the right and the largest on the left, so every number to the right of the decimal point has a value ten times smaller than its left-hand neighbor. The further it is to the right, the smaller it is. Numbers below units are described as tenths, hundredths, thousandths, and so on.

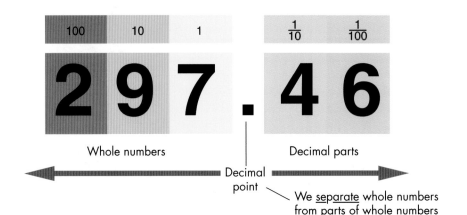

| 100 | 10 | 1 | | $\frac{1}{10}$ | $\frac{1}{100}$ |

2 9 7 . 4 6

Whole numbers   Decimal parts

Decimal point

We <u>separate</u> whole numbers from parts of whole numbers using a decimal point.

Florida working holiday

Randy had gone to Florida for a holiday. Since he did not have enough money to last for long, he needed to get a part-time job in a burger restaurant. His pay was $4.70 an hour. During the week he worked 17 hours.

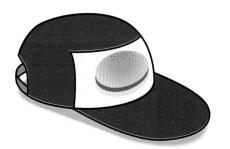

| 1,000 | 100 | 10 | 1 | $\frac{1}{10}$ | $\frac{1}{100}$ |

$ 4 . 7 0

Move numbers 2 places left

4 7 0 cents

Book link... To find out more about decimals, see the book *Decimals* in the *Math Matters!* set.

Setting out the problem

Before multiplying, change the decimal number into a whole number, thus changing $4.70 into 470 cents.

4.70 × 17 = ?

Put 470 above 17.

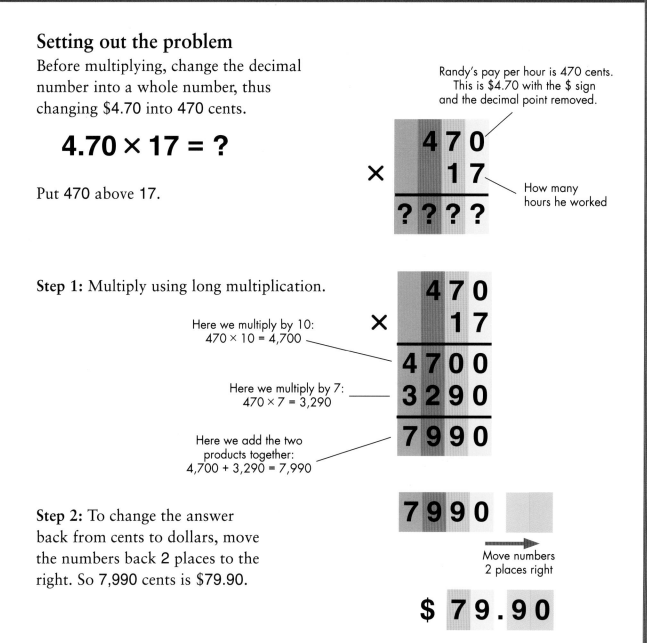

Randy's pay per hour is 470 cents. This is $4.70 with the $ sign and the decimal point removed.

$$\begin{array}{r} 470 \\ \times\ 17 \\ \hline ????\end{array}$$

How many hours he worked

Step 1: Multiply using long multiplication.

Here we multiply by 10: 470 × 10 = 4,700

Here we multiply by 7: 470 × 7 = 3,290

Here we add the two products together: 4,700 + 3,290 = 7,990

$$\begin{array}{r} 470 \\ \times\ 17 \\ \hline 4700 \\ 3290 \\ \hline 7990\end{array}$$

Step 2: To change the answer back from cents to dollars, move the numbers back 2 places to the right. So 7,990 cents is $79.90.

7990

Move numbers 2 places right

$ 79.90

Remember... To multiply two numbers when one is a decimal, do the multiplication without the decimal point, then put the decimal point back in the answer as many places from the right as it was in the original number.

Word check

Decimal number: A number that contains parts of units as well as whole units. The decimal point is used to separate the units from the parts of a unit.

Decimal place: The digits used for parts of a unit, such as tenths and hundredths. For example, if a number is given to "2 decimal places," it means that there are digits in the tenths and hundredths columns.

Decimal point: A dot written after the units when a number contains parts of a unit as well as whole numbers.

Finding an unknown amount

Multiplying, together with adding, can help you find unknown amounts in an equation.

The duke's lost cuff link

It was a bad day in Wellington Castle. The Duke of Bute was in a temper because he had lost a diamond cuff link.

Then he had an idea. He marched off to the nearby village and told the children what had happened.

"Two years' allowance and ten gold pieces," said he, "to the sharp-eyed, nimble-fingered whippersnapper who can find my cuff link." Gold pieces were used as money in his country in those days.

There was no shortage of searchers! He marched back to the ducal bedroom, followed by an army of children. They swarmed everywhere: under the bed, behind the curtains, on top of the wardrobe, in the wastepaper basket, all through the bedcovers – everywhere.

Finally, Willi Wiesel squeaked: "Here it is!" The duke had dropped the cuff link inside a wellington boot. The duke was overjoyed and gave Willi **34** gold pieces in a silk purse. How much do you think the duke figured a year's allowance was?

This is how we work it out

We have to write down how much the reward is in a number sentence:

"Two years' allowance and ten gold pieces comes to **34** gold pieces." Because we don't yet know what the duke thinks a year's allowance is, we have to leave a space to work it out. We have used a **?** below to show this unknown amount.

We can write the sentence again like this:

$$2 \times \boxed{?} + 10 = 34$$

We need to arrange for the **?** to be all on its own on the left-hand side of the equation.

First, take **10** from both sides (remember, if you do the same thing to both sides of an equation, you do not change the value of the equation).

The equation becomes:

so
$$2 \times \boxed{?} = 34 - 10$$
$$2 \times \boxed{?} = 24$$

Now divide both sides of our equation by **2**. That makes:

$$\boxed{?} = 24 \div 2$$
$$\boxed{?} = 12$$

Now we know that the duke thought that a year's allowance would be **12** gold pieces, or a gold piece a month.

Remember... This problem looked really hard, didn't it? But the answer was very simple. Remember, the first step is to convert words into an equation by putting a **?** for the unknown. Then you rearrange the equation to leave the **?** on its own.

What symbols mean

Here is a list of the common math symbols together with an example of how they are used. You will find this list in each of the *Math Matters!* books, so that you can turn to any book if you want to look up the meaning of a symbol.

— Between two numbers this symbol means "subtract" or "minus." In front of one number it means the number is negative. In Latin *minus* means "less."

= The symbol for equals. We say it "equals" or "makes." It comes from a Latin word meaning "level" because weighing scales are level when the amounts on each side are equal.

+ The symbol for adding. We say it "plus." In Latin *plus* means "more."

✗ The symbol for multiplying. We say it "multiplied by" or "times."

$$(8 + 9 - 3) \times \frac{2}{5} = 5.6$$

( ) Parentheses. You do everything inside the parentheses first. Parentheses always occur in pairs.

—, /, and ÷ Three symbols for dividing. We say it "divided by." A pair of numbers above and below a / or — make a fraction, so ⅖ or $\frac{2}{5}$ is the fraction two-fifths.

■ This is a decimal point. It is a dot written after the units when a number contains parts of a unit as well as whole numbers. This is the decimal number five point six or five and six-tenths.

Glossary

Terms commonly used in this book.

Adding: A quick way of counting.

Carrying: In adding or multiplying, when the working column total is bigger than 10, this is the method of adding the left digit at the bottom of the column on the left.

Column: Things placed one below the other.

Decimal number: A number that contains parts of units as well as whole units. The decimal point is used to separate the units from the parts of a unit.

Decimal place: The digits used for parts of a unit, such as tenths and hundredths. For example, if a number is given to "2 decimal places," it means that there are digits in the tenths and hundredths columns.

Decimal point: A dot written after the units when a number contains parts of a unit as well as whole numbers.

Digit: The numerals 1, 2, 3, 4, 5, 6, 7, 8, 9, or 0. Several may be used to stand for a larger number. They are called digits to make it clear that they are only part of a complete number. So we might say, "The second digit is 4," meaning the second numeral from the left. Or we might say, "That is a two-digit number," meaning that it has two numerals in it, tens and units.

Equals: The things on either side of an equals sign are the same.

Equation: A number sentence using the = symbol, telling us that two different ways of writing a number are the same. For example, $2 + 2 = 4$ and $9 - 5 = 4$.

Factor: A number used for multiplying.

Lots of: A common way of saying multiply.

Makes: A common word for equals.

Multiple: One of the numbers from the list of all products of the number.

Multiplication facts: The numbers produced by multiplying together numbers we use a lot, such as $3 \times 4 = 12$. They are facts we remember rather than work out each time. Some people also refer to these multiplication facts as multiplication tables.

Multiplication square: The multiplication tables arranged into a square shape.

Multiplication tables: Multiplication facts set out in columns.

Prime factor: A prime number being used as a factor.

Prime number: A number that is not a multiple of anything.

Product: The answer when two or more numbers are multiplied together.

Row: Things placed side by side.

Splitting-Up Rule: When two numbers are being multiplied, one of them can be split up into parts that are easier to multiply separately. The separate answers are then added together.

Square number: The number of a collection of objects that can be arranged in a square. It is the product of two equal numbers (for example, 16 is the square number produced from 4×4).

Square root: The number that, multiplied by itself, produces a square number.

Total: The answer to an adding problem.

Turn-Around Rule: When we add or multiply the same two numbers, the answer is the same no matter which of the numbers comes first (but it does not hold for subtracting or dividing).

Whole number: A number containing only complete units, not parts of units (it does not contain decimals or fractions).

Set index